Native Enough

Native Enough

Nina O'Leary

Makwa Enewed
East Lansing, Michigan

♾ The paper used in this publication meets the minimum requirements of ANSI/NISO Z39.48-1992 (R 1997) (Permanence of Paper).

Makwa Enewed
Michigan State University Press
East Lansing, Michigan 48823-5245

Printed and bound in the United States of America.

28 27 26 25 24 23 22 21 20 19   1 2 3 4 5 6 7 8 9 10

Library of Congress Control Number: 2017963183
ISBN 978-1-938065-05-7 (paperback)

Book and cover design by Matthew Rezac
Cover image © 2018 Nina O'Leary. All rights reserved.

Makwa Enewed is an imprint of the American Indian Studies Series at Michigan State University Press.

Gordon Henry, Series Editor

Makwa Enewed stands dedicated to books that encompass the varied views and perspectives of people working in American Indian communities. In that light, books published under the Makwa Enewed imprint rely less on formal academic critique, argument, methodology, and research conventions and more on experientially grounded views and perspectives on issues, activities, and developments in Indian Country.

While work published in Makwa Enewed may resound with certain personal, speculative, conversational, political, and/or social concerns of individuals and groups of individual American Indian people, in a larger sense such concerns and their delivery reflect the import, strength, uniqueness, and potential viability of the imprint.

The imprint will gather its strength from the voices of tribal leaders, community activists, and socially engaged Native people. Thus, each publication under the Makwa Enewed imprint will call forth from tribally based people and places, reminding readers of the varied beliefs and pressing interests of American Indian tribal people and communities.

Visit Michigan State University Press at www.msupress.org

Contents

Foreword

Heid E. Erdrich

All the beautiful people pictured in this book look Native to me. Perhaps that is because I am an Ojibwe and German-American woman born and raised as a member of the Turtle Mountain Band of Chippewa. I have never thought of Native American people as looking one way or being one way. Paging through *Native Enough*, all the round, brown, pale, sharp, soft, subtle, and distinct faces shine with the future. Whether they know it or not, they are a nation coming—as their ancestors dreamed. In this book, in their own words, they give us a sense of the complex nature of identity and the care with which they seek to live as Native people. At the same time, many of these students are careful to acknowledge that their lived experiences have not all been alike.

Natives are not all alike. As an educator, I have said that phrase thousands of times. *Natives are not all alike* could be the subtitle of this commanding collection of portraits and interviews from Nina O'Leary. These Native people attend colleges that uphold agreements between nations and states, agreements to repay long-delayed debt by waiving tuition to descendants of those who ceded the land where the colleges sit. There are many such students. There are so many, in fact, that they make up the largest single minority group on each campus. But there is nothing singular about them—the umbrella term "Native American," held out to cover dozens of tribes, nations, cultures, and identities, does not fit all.

Statements that accompany their images, show their stances toward Native identity, are as varied as their faces. Many reveal they are proud, culturally engaged, comfortable with their identity. Yet just as many show they have been uncomfortable, uneasy, dislocated, or disturbed by the treatment of white students or other communities of color on campus, and even other Native students they encounter. Many also express, through reflection on their experiences at college, that they are exploring and growing into their identities. This is a time I remember well, a time in which all young people forge identities outside of their parents' or caregivers' sphere. But for Native students the experience can be complicated and challenging.

Native college students find themselves—and often for the first time—outside of their reservation and other Native communities. Such an experience can be dislocating, and equally so for the student who "looks Indian" as it can be for those who do not present as Native. In the larger world, these young people are beyond their lived context, beyond the aunts, uncles, grandparents, siblings, and others who know them and share culture. At the same time, for some Native students who have lived in the mainstream, far from Native family, college might be a first chance to explore being Native in the twenty-first century within a community of Native peers. That these first-time experiences happen at colleges where the atmosphere is one of growth and learning is not a bad thing. It is complex, it is often painful, and it is seemingly inescapable, as O'Leary portrays, but these college confrontations of identity are also clearly valued and supported.

The continuum of Native American experience is as enormously diverse. Over 566 Native nations comprise those living in the United States who are members of federally recognized tribes. To most Americans, and to the mainstream and international students who come to these colleges in significant numbers, notions of who Natives are can be limited, stereotyped, and narrowed by prejudice. Within that context Native students must deal with their peers' ignorant comments, and worse, their outright envy of the tuition waivers these students' ancestors paid in advance.

Think about that. Our ancestors paid in advance. They provided a legacy. Natives should be thanked, not made to think a favor is being done them. In that spirit, I've decided not to refer to a "tuition waiver" but to call it PRE-PAID TUITION. Our ancestors, elders to people I knew as a child, those who came before us pre-paid tuition at Morris and colleges like it. They pre-paid it with the land the school occupies.

My own family has a history with one of these institutions, the University of Minnesota Morris. Members of my family, both Ojibwe and Dakota, enrolled and descendants, have attended Morris recently and others plan to soon. We also have a history with Indian boarding schools, which, O'Leary explains, is what Morris was in the earlier century. My family went to such boarding schools (both government and mission), my maternal grandfather, my mother, some of my aunts, uncles, and cousins. My parents taught at a Bureau of Indian Affairs boarding school at Wahpeton, North Dakota, not far from Morris. My earliest memories are on the campus of an Indian boarding school. It looked a lot like the oldest parts of University of Minnesota Morris. The prairie and small-town features are familiar to me and it is not at all difficult for me to imagine what day-to-day life must be like for the students who O'Leary has photographed.

When I look at the portraits in this book, I see relatives. These faces could be the faces of a dozen dear, young (and sometimes older) people I have known who attended Morris. They chose the college not only because of our pre-paid tuition, but because it creates an excellent environment for Native American studies and promotes a cultural emphasis in student life. Pre-paid tuition has been a huge draw to many Native families I know across four states. Morris has become a tradition for Native families and, as I imagine from statements in this book, the same is true for Fort Lewis. Families have come to count on the possibility of an excellent education with a huge benefit. The only drawback, it seems, is that it places Native students in a complicated context with their peers.

It is hard to explain the context of Native student life at these land grant institutions, and *Native Enough* has taken on the task of telling it through single images and brief statements. To help the reader focus, O'Leary has organized the book around six themes that allow us understand the implications voiced by the students in these portraits: beginning with references to the contentious reality that most tribes enroll though identification of an individual's percentage of tribal inheritance (blood quantum), moving through difficulties students encounter (identity/anxiety) and the related experience of dealing with other's expectations (stereotypes), before ending with more culturally specific concerns (tribal issues) and the legacy of Indian boarding schools and education (school), to end with hopeful sections (things we love and getting in touch) that reveal more positive self-images and a keen interest in engaging Native cultures and identities.

Much of what these students say makes me uneasy. I worry that they feel they must reference something called "Native" rather than their own specific cultures and tribes. I worry that they feel they must justify their right to pre-paid tuition and to education itself. In some cases, I sense a deep unease with asserting their own existence as people of their tribes. It should not be this way. These colleges and all educators could, as a core value, assert and acknowledge that the generosity and forethought of the tribes allow these institutions to exist.

We too exist, these student portraits say. We do not get things "for free"—instead, our ancestors paid with our land, their mother. We hurt, these interviews say. We sometimes exclude one another, we are made ashamed of who we are and where we come from, we deal with social issues in our communities, problems we cannot entirely leave behind. But we love being together, we have traditions to uphold, we hope to negotiate food insecurity and protect Indigenous food-ways, we are excited to learn about media representation, Indigenous feminism, to continue our art and spiritual practice, and no matter what a challenge it is to be a Native student at a land grant institution, we love our cultures and learning about our histories in the larger national context. This knowledge that we are many is what keeps us going.

You are a legacy, is what I want to say to them.

When I look at these Native faces, when I read these strong statements in Native voices, I am filled with a pride so huge it could wipe away any anxiety Native students have ever been made to suffer. I hope the students pictured here read these words and are filled with a sense of rightfulness and purpose. Your ancestors and elders thought of you when they negotiated around the grant of land to create these schools. They dreamed you in all your thousands of distinct ways of being in the world. And they counted on you as the nation they saw coming.

If anyone ever bugs you about how you look or why your tuition was pre-paid, just point to this book. There are thousands of permutations of Native American identity and each has a face. These photos by Nina O'Leary are a few gorgeous examples.

Acknowledgments

Students at University of Minnesota, Morris, and Fort Lewis College: Thank you for trusting me with your stories. I know we spoke in a fleeting time of life, and by the time this is published you very well might not be in the same place as you were. Trust that because you chose to openly process identity with me, your questions and thoughts will resonate with some readers. I don't think we will ever quite figure identity out, but your honesty with me was and is priceless and will touch many. Know that every conversation, at the very least, helped me along in my journey to understanding Native identity and self. I am forever grateful.

Becca Gercken and Jess Larson at the University of Minnesota, Morris: Thank you for always believing in me, often more than I believed in myself. Your advice and insight throughout the project has been absolutely invaluable.

Julie Loehr at Michigan State University Press: Thank you for seeing my intent with this project from the very beginning so clearly. I am forever grateful that you believed in the work enough to publish it.

Heid Erdrich: Thank you for the beautiful foreword. You are my favorite Native poet and writer and I feel so lucky to have your words associated with my work.

Elizabeth Mason, President Dene Thomas, Yvonne Bilinski, Mariah Gachupin, and Stephanie Lefthand at Fort Lewis College: For your hospitality, flexibility, and welcoming spirit.

Lynn Lukkas, Monica Haller, Paul Shambroom, and Christine Baeumler at the University of Minnesota.

Mary Modeen at Duncan of Jordanstone College of Art, Dundee, Scotland.

Matthew Rezac: For taking the project to a new level with your incredible design.

Matt O'Leary: For listening to this little idea I had over Subway sandwiches in Morris and believing in me the whole way through. I love you.

Becca Haider: For your insight in organizing stories and faces in the most compelling way, and for your ever-honest and enthusiastic feedback throughout the process.

Matt O'Leary, Emily Steward, Donna Berg, John & Johanna Franey, Dan Tiernan, Jenna Ray, and Kurtis & Becca Haider: For your extra eyes on the introduction.

Introduction

I never thought much about what being Native American meant before college. My family is a bit of a melting pot, so being Native felt about as important as being Danish, Sicilian, Welsh, or anything else in our expansive gene pool. Our connection to Cherokee life-ways was nonexistent, and most of us had never been to the reservation. I was relatively ignorant of that history, but I knew it was something true about me—and I left it at that.

These ideas resurfaced during my college search after my mom and I trekked up to the University of Minnesota, Morris (UMM), on a whim. I instantly grew attached to the brick buildings and homey feel of the campus, along with an enthusiastic admissions officer, who casually handed me an informational brochure. On the very back page, in small type, was UMM's tuition waiver for Native American students. My mom assumed I wouldn't qualify since our blood quantum was below most standards to receive scholarships, but after gathering all of the necessary family documents, I did.

Although I never questioned my ancestry or the documents tracing my family back to the Trail of Tears, I felt uncomfortable suddenly identifying as Native at UMM. My lack of stereotypically phenotypic Native features fueled my self-doubt. If other Native students discovered my pseudo-secret, I feared they'd call me a fraud. I was in hiding. After years of learning more about my tribe and the current issues facing indigenous peoples across the nation and world, I gradually embraced my identity as a Cherokee person—and I now feel totally confident in this piece of myself. There are still moments of uneasiness—fear of being found out for having a low blood quantum while identifying so strongly as Native. It doesn't help that I am Cherokee, the tribe that is most commonly falsely claimed.

I began to explore my insecurities regarding the waiver more deeply following a rocky junior-year review in my Studio Art program. My professors criticized my work for lacking any personal elements or the honesty I truly thought it had. After a summer of licking my artist-ego wounds, I returned for my senior year of undergraduate classes intending to pursue an urgently personal idea: the "Native Enough" project.

Process

The project can be concisely explained as a representation of an experiential and phenotypic spectrum of the Native college student, and exists as a collection of portraits paired with excerpts from interviews done with the students immediately before taking their portraits. My goal was to illustrate to Natives and non-Natives that there is not just one way to think or look Native. To me, the portraits and interviews combined are experiential portraits.

Many people's ingrained images of Native Americans begin with Edward Curtis, a late nineteenth-century American photographer who produced a large body of work, often of Native subjects. Because Curtis was convinced that Natives and their cultures were about to disappear, he persuaded his subjects to wear full regalia (often not even from their own tribe) and to hide any markers of cultural adaptation such as clocks, iron cookware, and so on. While many people in the field of American Indian Studies and some in art history are aware of how staged his photographs were, the general public is not. Natives exist(ed) in many more styles of dress than ceremonial regalia, which isn't clear from only seeing Curtis's work. These negative representations are made more problematic by the fact that his pictures remain in wide circulation.

I wanted the images in this book to disrupt the notions that Curtis's work has instilled in our society by creating current images of Native students. When I first started taking steps to make the visual component of this project a reality, I did an outdoor photo shoot with a student at UMM in her ceremonial regalia. Even though this was the student's own self-made powwow regalia, the image seemed to perpetuate the Curtis-based stereotypes of Native people I set out to work against. A lone Native woman wearing braids and a jingle dress in the middle of a field didn't exactly meet my goal of reminding viewers that Natives are very much still here, part of contemporary society. I was inspired to change my approach, and for the remainder of the experiential portraits, my subjects wore whatever they wanted and said whatever was on their minds, instead of being directed to put on traditional garments and remain the stoic, unfeeling and unspeaking Indians of the art world's past. I wanted the project to challenge the general tendency for Native and non-Native

people to disqualify individuals from identifying with their culture because they don't look Native enough—to assert that neither the assumptions of popular culture nor even those of fellow Natives determine Native identity. The final photographs are simple portraits on a white background, converted to black and white as a response to Curtis's images. My aesthetic solution was inspired by Richard Avedon's signature style of photographing people in front of a stark white background, removing any context for who they might be other than how they choose to present themselves.

Once I clarified the visual language of the project for myself, I sent out a mass e-mail to all of the students on the waiver at UMM, sharing my stories and asking for volunteers who might like to talk with me and have a quick portrait taken. I got hundreds of responses within the first day—students jumped at the chance to be able to talk about something that was rarely publicly discussed on campus. I started meeting with my peers and asking them a series of questions regarding their background, upbringing, and experience with sharing or hiding their identity with others. Interview after interview, my suspicions were confirmed. While there were many students at UMM who felt extremely secure and confident in their culture, the majority either felt guilty for identifying with their heritage or expressed that they tried to keep it under wraps in order to avoid dealing all-too-common peer responses: "You don't look Native enough!" "How much are you?" "You can't be Native because . . ." Many felt exhausted from fielding these responses and quietly resigned from fighting the stereotypes. How often can you be told by others that you simply can't identify with a part of your heritage before you start to believe it?

I was aware that the framing of my questions would have a powerful effect on the responses of the participants, so I made sure to choose them carefully. My questions ranged from specific, focused questions like "have you ever experienced negative reactions (including jokes) to your Native identity based on the way that you look," to more vague, positively focused questions like "what is your favorite part about your tribe's culture?" I started with general questions to help me understand the participant's background, and then continued asking questions until I hit something that sparked emotion, passion, or introspection in them. Once we reached those moments together, I knew that I could move on to the next portion of the project.

After interviewing each person, I spent less than a minute capturing their portrait. It was important to me that I spent time getting to know each individual before photographing them in order to ensure that their interview excerpt would correctly inform the viewer's reading of their image. These portraits as individual images not only effectively reinforce the concept that phenotype is not a reliable indicator of Indian-ness, but they also paint a more accurate picture of the spectrum of Native experience and phenotype than media and pop culture stereotypes.

The Universities

I spent almost my whole senior year at UMM (2014–2015) photographing and interviewing students. I traveled to Fort Lewis College (FLC) in Durango, Colorado, in October of 2015 to continue, and returned to Morris for the final portion in the spring of 2016 as an artist-in-residence.[1]

While UMM and FLC have similar historical origins and share a current public liberal arts mission, their student bodies, and thus the experiences of their indigenous students, are quite different. UMM is on the site of a residential school first run by the Sisters of Mercy and later run by the federal government. The tuition waiver is for any American Indian or First Nations student who can document their Native heritage. Official UMM policy defines an American Indian as follows:

- "an enrolled member of a federally recognized American Indian tribe, Alaskan Native Village, or Canadian First Nation;
- a direct descendant of a parent or grandparent who is an enrolled member of a federally recognized American Indian tribe, Alaskan Native Village, or Canadian First Nation; or
- a direct descendant of a tribally verified member of a federally recognized American Indian tribe, Alaskan Native Village, or Canadian First Nation, other than parent or grandparent."[2]

FLC was originally an army base that was converted to a residential school in 1891. Eventually the deed for the land was transferred to the state, with nearly the same conditions as UMM.[3] The waiver, fittingly, is almost identical: "To qualify, you must: 1. Have your own enrollment or census number; or 2. Provide documentation that you are 50% Native American; or 3. Prove you are a direct descendant of a tribal member who, on June 1, 1934, resided within the present boundaries of any Native American reservation."[4]

Since most universities in the United States only give designated financial assistance to students who have a specified high blood quantum, UMM and FLC stand apart in the variety of students allowed to receive financial benefit due to their indigeneity.

When I was photographing students at Morris from 2014 to 2016, Native students made up 17% of the student body, and there were 2 Native student groups out of 127 total. When I visited in 2015, 33% of students at FLC were Native American, and 16% of their student groups were focused on Native identity, pride, and activism.

My trip to FLC perfectly coincided with a vibrant and active indigenous people's festival on campus, so I was able to share a bit about my project there. However, I mainly relied on a mass e-mail sent out to the Native student population before my visit and word of mouth to advertise my project. I interviewed and photographed 43 students in 2.5 days there—about the same amount that I did in UMM over a span of about 7 months during my senior year. This book includes every person and story that I heard during the project, with nobody emitted, for a total of 109 portraits and interviews.

My choice to only include Native college students at land-grant institutions with a waiver was a simple way to ensure that the students that I spoke to had proven their indigeneity to their respective universities—removing me from the uncomfortable position of judging others' Native-ness. While this book is finished, I don't think the project's goal will ever be. I will continue to make art exploring my own identity as a Cherokee and encouraging others to grapple with, celebrate, and live out their indigeneity.

It has been an honor to hear stories, share laughs, and talk through tears with the students from the University of Minnesota, Morris and Fort Lewis College who volunteered to be a part of this book. I am forever thankful.

Notes

1. The third university that I hoped to work with was Haskell Indian Nations University in Lawrence, Kansas. Haskell requires students to be enrolled in a federally recognized tribe or at least one-quarter Native American to attend. I anticipated conversations there to be very different from those at UMM or Fort Lewis, which have more lenient standards on who can attend on the waiver. Although faculty expressed interest at my initial contact, I did not receive any response afterward from anyone at the university during my two years of attempts.

2. Https://policy.umn.edu/morris/amindianwaiver.

3. Https://www.fortlewis.edu/master-plan/ ExistingConditions/HistoryofFortLewisCollege.aspx.

4. Https://www.fortlewis.edu/Portals/0/ FLC-Certificate-Indian-Blood-2017.pdf.

Native Enough

Hunter: I think about the philosophy, what's the essence of being Native? Is it just the fact that you're related, or is it characteristics and ideals to live up to?

Nicole: It's not about how somebody looks, it's how they feel inside. Although, people might feel like they are Native, but when you have no connection, no understanding of the culture, no understanding of the struggles of Native people, that's hard. It's hard when they claim Native identity because it's cool or exotic or trendy, but not because they care. I've had some friends who are white who say "My great-great-grandma is Cherokee but I never claim that because I don't know what it means." When people pretend to know what that means, I find that insulting. If you're helping, if you're a productive contributor to the forward movement of indigenous peoples, that's when it's okay. Otherwise, you can be an ally. It's important for indigenous peoples to have non-Native allies.

Mikaylah: I like the history. I've always been interested in Indians, I think it's cool.

Francis: Growing up in a non-traditional Native American home I never felt like I was Native American. Maybe that's because I bought into the stereotypical idealization of what it means to be Native. I've been assimilated but I'm still reaching out to my culture. "Native American" isn't some gold standard to live up to, it's something we define ourselves by every day.

Perry: I had the benefit of knowing people who knew culture and language, and I grew up on the reservation. Most Natives that I've met don't live on reservations, so it's cool to see them eager to learn about the culture.

← **Annie:** I remember in gym class a really light skinned girl with bleach blonde hair called me a honky because she thought I was too white. She practiced more traditional ways so she thought she was more Native than me. It's hard to base someone's identity off of the way they look.

→ **Laura:** I'm Cherokee, and ultimately because the Cherokees have open enrollment and whatnot, a lot of folks that phenotypically don't look Native identify as such. And they're super flippant about their involvement which is really harmful, you know, when celebrities and people who aren't actually enrolled are like "Oh yeah, my great-grandma was a Cherokee princess!" It's like, dude, not even a thing. Didn't actually happen. If I'm with a large group of Native folks, I won't even identify as Cherokee because it's those white folks that identify as Cherokee who are messing it up for those of us who really are.

Autumn: I don't look Native, so I think that people might be offended if I do identify with it. There's a lot of hurt and suffering in those communities that I haven't experienced, so I might not have the right to claim that as my culture.

Larie: I think being Native and being connected to your people is very important. If you grew up in an urban place and you only know that you're Native, that's not your fault! There's nothing wrong with trying to figure out where you're from.

Alle: I love the percussion at powwows, but I would never be able to perform in that because it's done by males. I respect the patriarchy of that ritual, but I wish I could be one of the drummers.

Max: My mom is the Native one. All of her brothers and sisters were enrolled, but she was born one year after the cutoff. She's not an official member of the tribe so neither are my sister Alle and I. Feeling left out and not being able to enroll kind of sucks. It's like an exclusive club, and all the members are dying out.

Michelle: Catholic boarding schools typically recruited from one reservation. Morris recruited from my tribe, Turtle Mountain. The moment it hit me—oh my god, my grandmother went here—was a holy shit moment. If you think about the cyclical memory of Native people, I feel like somehow by coming here and re-learning my culture and language, that it's healing that past wound. It was mind blowing the moment I realized that.

Briana: Some family members say that I'm not Native enough. They have darker skin, so somehow they feel that my family isn't as Native as them. We are equal amounts Native if you look at blood quantum.

← **Tony:** My grandma was given up for adoption, and there's dispute over how much Native blood I have. My blood quantum could well be higher than it is—I think I'm only counted at like 8 percent or something crazy low—but everyone on my grandma's side was born and raised on the res. So, when people ask me my opinion on blood quantum, I refer to it as paper genocide. It's a way to further thin out our numbers based on some arbitrary genetic or birth record–based notion. I think it's more a question of self-identity. It's not what I look like on the outside. I get to define what I am and how I feel about it.

→ **Jessica:** I feel that it's a bit of a hindrance that I don't look Native when I'm trying to learn about it and when I talk to other Natives that look it. They think "Just another white person trying to learn about us," but then I tell them that I'm Native too and they tend to be taken aback slightly. It's not judgment, it's more restrictive questions—they know I'm Native but they're trying to figure how Native I am (however you figure that out).

Emma: The one-drop policy weirds me out. If you're the tiniest bit Native, you're white—which is the opposite of what it was for African Americans (one drop of African American blood, and that meant you were black).

Jesse: It's kind of given me an interesting perspective on my family because we didn't get it officially documented until a few years ago. It's in my dad's line, but his mom doesn't like talking about it. From my grandma and generations before her, they're all trying to keep it hush hush.

Bethany: It's weird when people ask about blood quantum—as if it's not a personal question! When you say "I'm Native" and they're like "Oh, one thirty-second?" With other minorities, at what point do you stop being Black or Asian? There's not a point. There's no limit. It's just a way for the government to get us down to say "You're not your own nation anymore, we don't have to follow these treaty rights anymore." When I talk to some Natives at Morris, most of them think the blood quantum is dumb, but I know there are people out there who think otherwise.

Travis: I am Native American. I've been involved in my culture since elementary school. I was told that I did not have enough blood to receive the waiver at Morris, initially. I did end up getting it, and had much gratitude. From the experience of being told I was not enough, I felt that I needed to be very quiet about it so students with and without the waiver would not ostracize me. Today, I still question if the Native American community genuinely accepts me. I've grown tired of feeling that I should hide my Native American background.

JoMarie: I don't think being enrolled in a tribe says how Indian you are. Or your blood quantum—how can they go inside your body and tell? It's how you live your life and how you feel inside. We're the only people in the country that have to prove who we are and that's not right.

Joseph: I do not believe in blood quantum, that is a foreign concept imposed upon us to weed us out. What percentage of me is Native, or white? The whole idea is fucked-up, it makes me feel like a dog with papers.

Olivia: If they find out, they say "But you're a white girl!"

Identity/Anxiety

Decide which photo pairs with which statement.
(*Answer key on page 130.*)

I feel like if I do tell people I'm Native, they're going to ask me about my culture, and I have no idea. I feel like I should find out more and get involved with Native life on campus, but I'd be worried about reactions to my fair skin in those circles.

I'm quick to tell others about my Native identity, because it's who I am.

I feel kind of like a traitor when I go to powwows, because I'm Native but I'm also white. I don't "look" Native.

I feel proud to be Native, but I do not feel like I look it. I feel a little guilty when talking to "more pure" Native Americans regarding my relationship to being Native. I just enjoy my Native side, even looking dominantly white.

← **Richard:** Being in Morris, there are so many people that are "white" Native Americans, more than I would think. I don't think I could go to a more Native American school, based on how many there are [at Fort Lewis College]. I probably wouldn't want to. I would feel uncomfortable there.

→ **Fidel:** To be honest, I don't know what it means to be Native sometimes. The language is the only thing that's part of me that makes me feel Native. Growing up in Christianity, I was always told it was either white man's belief or it was seen as bad. In school kids would say "Well, you're a Christian, should you be doing ceremonies?" But when you're in church, they say "You're not supposed to be doing ceremonies and using peyote, that's witchcraft!"

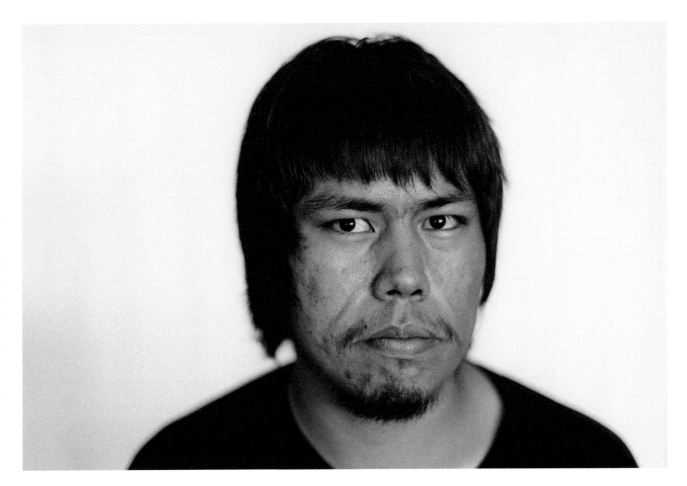

Virginia: I didn't say I was Native in middle and high school because all through those years people said I was the "white girl that played Native." They said I couldn't be Native because I'm white—so I had to keep that part of myself hidden.

Nicole: It's funny, in high school I said I was Native to two boys and they said "No you're not" and they called me a fake Indian for a while. I got a little offended, but I didn't know how to respond. I'm still on that journey to understanding what that means. One of those guys is here at Fort Lewis on waiver, and I'm like, "Yeah, I got it too." He told his friend and they thought it was so funny. I didn't realize the implications of what they were saying and how that affected me and how I identify.

Luke: People joke around with me when they find out that I'm Native. I'm not offended, but I do feel like a hypocrite sometimes, and I feel like I'm taking advantage of it because I don't identify culturally as much as others. I don't hold a lot of cultural traits or habits that people that look or identify strongly as Native have.

Sarah: I'm an enrolled member of the White Earth reservation, but I don't look Native American at all. So, it's like, do I go with who I am on the inside or what I look like on the outside?

Amber: Can I really truly see myself as Native? I've identified as white for so long, if I claim Native-ness, there's more people saying I can't than I can. I don't look Native, and anytime I do say it, it turns into an argument about why I can't be or that I'm lying.

← **Alayna:** There is a lot of ongoing tension between Native and non-Native communities where I'm from, so I often had reluctance to identify as such unless I felt I was with accepting people. Other times, people just flat-out denied that I was Native if I told them, often times including racist stereotypes as justification, which was always painful. Despite this, I've learned not to let other people's prejudices and ignorance influence something as personal to me as my identity and my relationship with those who came before me. It's something that's deeply important to me and that's what should matter.

→ **Elizabeth:** I grew up with the white half of my family, who are Mormons. They did a lot of cultural erasure of indigenous people and ignored that part of me until it came to health care, because of course they didn't want to pay a penny for that. I'm trying to reclaim something that was never offered to me. I feel wronged, because nobody in my family thought I should be taught the stories or the culture.

Tyler: My father was raised white—you didn't want to be Native because people were really racist. So, he raised me in the white way too. I guess this year I was having trouble finding my spirituality because I was raised white. Because yeah, I was raised white, but I wouldn't say I'm a Christian. If I was any spirituality it would be Native. But I don't go to ceremonies or do traditional things, so I don't know, I kind of just float. But it's not a terrible thing to be in the middle.

Adrianna: Knowing about the history and all the terrible things that happened makes me hurt. I researched a lot about boarding schools last year and it was really hard knowing that one religion or the majority population just determined this is how things are going to be. I'm Catholic too, and trying to find the balance there is really hard. It's weird, people say "Oh well you can't really be Catholic and also be Native, because it's like night and day!" But my family found a way to stay true to Native culture and Catholic religion.

Katharine: I try to keep a respectful distance from Native identity because I can't claim it as much, being a white girl! I don't want to invade that space. I have privilege because I'm white, people who look more Native don't get to occupy that privileged space. But it's not an accident that I look white, it's a result of the systematic degradation and dismissal of Native American culture. Sometimes I think about my full blood great-great-grandma, I hear stories of what she went through, and that's no accident. The history of my whiteness is important.

Alven: White privilege? Your family got set back! Your family wasn't rich. We started out in Oklahoma on a pile of rocks, dirt poor, and now we're here! Look how far you came. If that hadn't happened, where would you be today? Monetarily? Real estate? You might've been going to Notre Dame! You're that far behind! At some point, you got set back! Where was that white privilege when they chose to throw you on the stockade? When they looked at the Native in you and not the white?

Addison: I love being Alaskan Native. People think "Oh, Eskimo!" and that's not it. I'm Aleut technically. In World War II my ancestors were sent to internment camps because our descent is Mongolian, Russian, and Japanese. A lot of our population died and it was shoved under the rug. Then in the late '80s or '90s Bill Clinton was like "our bad" and sent dispersion checks to the remaining survivors.

Kayla: I love the culture but I feel guilty for identifying with it. I feel guilty talking to "real Natives." People always told me to check "white" and that hurt my identity. I was talking to a Native girl once and at first she thought I was legit, but then I told her I was mostly black.

← **Andrew:** I've struggled my whole life to cope with the fact that I'm Native, and to be proud of it. I still question if I like being Native or not because it's really not that big of a deal in my life. I'm just in a state of mind where I want to learn new things and meet new people. I'm descended from Native Americans and some French guys. It's just a piece of who I am.

→ **Brandi:** I'm Vietnamese and Native American, but everyone thinks I'm full blown Asian or something. Since I don't look Vietnamese those people treat me differently, but since I don't look Native they treat me differently. I grew up with Buddhist temples and Sunday school, but I didn't know anything about my Native side. I got made fun of when I was a kid for my last name, it was Scarcehawk. In high school it got changed to Nguyen. It used to be that if people would ask me in K–12 I'd just say I was Asian. Now that I'm here learning about being Native, I say that I'm both.

Andrea: I am biracial, and I've found that White/Native individuals can identify with either race depending on the context of their situation. In Morris I feel more Native American and I feel closer to my Native self because issues and life ways are celebrated here. But when I go home, it's a different story. The dominant majority was Native at home, but they were all looked down on and profiled in my town. I always was embarrassed because of the negativity towards them to share what part of my race was. I'd just say I'm white. I feel for my Native peers here who have had trouble with racist attitudes against them, but I can't totally relate because I have some white privilege. I can hide behind my white skin, so I haven't had those experiences. I try not to do that now. I don't want to be one or the other because it's convenient. I just want to be both.

Rachel: I know I look white but I'm actually Native. Usually I'm so anxious that I offer it up before they can even say anything. I'm Native and Spanish, but both cultures I'm torn between . . . I'm not a part of either, too white for either. I'm not really sure where I go. There are times when I've been like, I'm too white to be Native! I guess I'm anxious that I'll meet someone who will tell that to me, but so far, I haven't.

Jandrea: I think about applying for jobs, when they ask you your race . . . I look white and I do identify with that, but I want to put Native American to help me stand out above the rest of the pile. But I also know that when someone is looking at my application they're going to put an identity on me, on how I look, my work ethic and the stereotypes that come with that.

_____

Decide which photo pairs with which statement.
(*Answer key on page 130.*)

I've heard that because I'm a Native woman I couldn't be trusted. People have made alcoholism jokes, tuition waiver jokes, free money jokes. I wish I could educate the public better and fight racism and stereotypes.

I have to specify what kind of Indian I am. They assume "red dot." One of my friends thought that I was from India for a really long time.

I'm from a tribe in the Vermont area. All of my best girl friends were Menomonie, but they just saw me as a white friend.

The questions aren't "Tell us about your culture," they're "Tell us what you gain monetarily from it?"

Michelle: I dated a really Native person, and one time his dad was like, "I wish you would find a really nice Native girl." It was so hurtful. I felt like all the shit my mom went through and the hardships that my grandpa and aunts and uncles faced didn't even matter because of the way that I look.

_____

Jordan: I want to eliminate the idea that we don't exist anymore. In Europe, they thought I was Filipino. I was the only Native they'd ever known or seen. But there's Natives everywhere! In New York, this guy was looking at us really weird and my cousin said "Can I help you?" He said "Where are you from?" She said New Mexico, and he was like, "But what are you?" When he found out we were Native American he said "I've only heard about Natives in history books!" For me it's about making sure people know we are here and just as "civil" as they are.

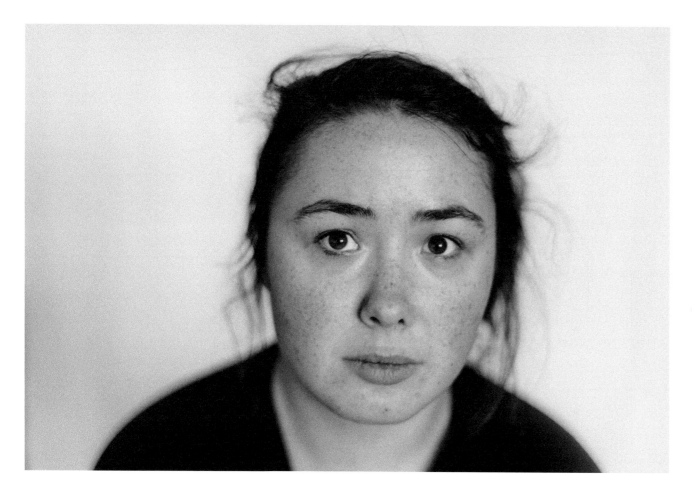

Olivia: Stereotypes that are affiliated with being Native, and especially being Alaska Native, are really bad. People say the Natives are all drunks, they have no purpose in life, they don't have good education. In Alaska, it's especially harsh in public schools. I look at it as motivation, I'm definitely going to change that!

Stacy: I was in the Air Force for five years before college. I was the only Native working in my squadron or maybe on base. This guy referred to me as a squaw. He was joking and laughing but I was like, that's not nice. At the time I was very young, maybe nineteen, so I didn't think much of it. But I remember it.

← **Sabrina:** Wearing feathers . . . I don't know. I don't know why they are always associated with Natives. I understand why a headdress is sacred. I'm not trying to offend anyone by wearing feather earrings, if I was trying to offend I'd get a Hitler mustache. I understand that they got stomped on by white people, but I'm a little bit Native so I don't see the problem.

→ **Sunni:** In middle school when I left for a week-long coming of age ceremony, people thought I was sacrificed to my tribe! They made all kinds of remarks about it. It made me so uncomfortable, but they thought it was funny.

Jolena: People think I get everything for free, and at FLC it's been made known that some people don't like that we get our tuition waived. People think we're favored. If they looked back at the history, they'd realize we've never been favored! I guarantee people who think we are favored have never been on a reservation.

Savanna: I don't like people thinking everything is handed to us because we're Native, with IHS [Indian Health Service] and the waiver. They don't realize we get really low coverage and expired medications. They don't realize how much trauma Native people went through, and that what the government is doing now to help doesn't make up for what they caused in the first place.

← **Breanna:** My sister Bethany and I were really light when we were younger—we had platinum blonde hair. We have darker hair now so we don't get crap for it. We live on the Cheyenne River Reservation, and people were like "Oh my god what are these little white girls doing on our reservation?" We weren't allowed to dance in our own culture because people were against it based on how blonde and pale we were. I just don't understand how people think, "Oh you're not dark, you're not a part of this ethnicity." You really don't understand what the culture is about if you think it's all based on features.

→ **Demi:** I had a white kid who grew up around the lower Sioux community say "You're welcome" to me for getting the waiver. I was like, "You know it's from boarding schools, right?" And he was like "You're welcome for the boarding schools too." That made me feel really weird. I mean, we're friends, but we butt heads when it comes to that stuff a lot.

← **Amanda:** I got a lot of negative tones from people (at Morris) who found out I had the waiver. I'm not confrontational, so it made me take a few steps back and I felt bad for being Native. But the more I got used to Morris and knew about it the prouder I got. I got salty about people judging me for the waiver. The more people said it, the more stupid it sounded. So, you're judging me based on my culture and my race, but not who I actually am?

→ **Nancy:** Sometimes when I bring it up to white people, they go "Ugh, you get the tuition waiver." Then they say "This might sound bad, but I wish there was a way to figure out if I'm Native or not," which is tokenizing the situation. Like "Oh, Natives, they don't have to pay for stuff." That's all they care about, they don't care that it's some people's pride.

Kaitlyn: I feel like if I don't get a degree or if I drop out, if I become a teen mother, I'll just become another statistic. When I was in grade school and middle school, a lot of the adults, counselors, teachers, aunts and uncles shoved it down my throat. Like, this percent doesn't graduate high school or college. I got it drilled into my head and I knew I didn't want to be that. Not only was I hearing it all the time, but I was watching my friends dropping out of high school and becoming teen mothers. I wanted to be different than that.

Courtney: I'm one of fifteen out of my graduating class that doesn't have a baby right now. I graduated in a class of 105. A lot of my classmates started having kids really young. It's always been a thing in the back of my head to tell my cousins, "Slow your roll! Enjoy being who you are first."

Cassondra: Living in an urban area can be sad because you want to be a part of your Native American community but at the same some of the reservations don't even have running water—and you wouldn't want to live there. How do you find the culture without getting brought into everything else, the negative things?

Sidney: I think a challenge that we face is the loss of our language. It does a lot for our identities as Native people. We interpret our life through our language, and if we don't have that we can't really be ourselves. But nobody really cares to learn the language lately.

_____

Veronica: I'm taking Anishinaabe classes here, and it's been super exciting bringing that back home to my family and sharing it with them. Sometimes I speak some to my grandpa and he remembers bits and pieces. It brings him to tears.

Dylan: When I was learning Dakota, it was just me and one other person, and he was a tribal member. So, there wasn't a lot of people to practice with and I kind of lost it over the years. Now they're doing a program in the elementary school to teach them the language right away so they can all practice together. My little cousin speaks really well!

Jasmine: I was in a Native group in high school, and we were vicious to newcomers. This new girl came and we asked to see her papers, we said she wasn't Native enough and said she couldn't join us. Maybe it's a pushback against white supremacy, us saying "This is something special!" We're a minority, if you're not a percentage enough then you're not a part of us! But Native to Native, we can't do that to each other. It's so true, I'm not anxious to tell someone who's not Native that I'm Native, but I'm scared to tell a Native that I'm Native. There has been a shift from cultural values to shaming each other.

Braeden: It's kind of hard here because the majority of Native students at Morris are Lakota and there's this weird rivalry between us and them. I'd go to Native school clubs and they'd slander Ojibwe people. I was like, this is ridiculous, we should be working together! I don't go anymore.

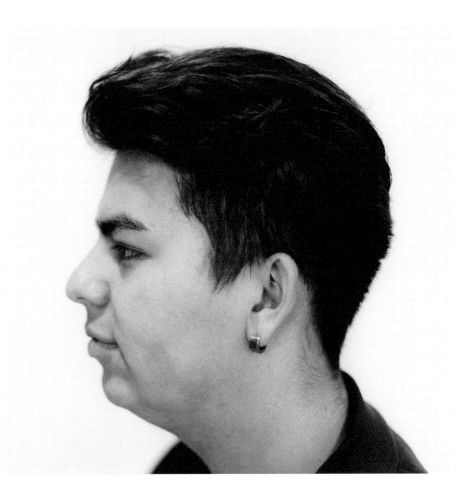

Nicole: I'm trying to get involved with everything I can to raise awareness about sexual assault against indigenous women. A lot of my family members have experienced this, and we all bond over this subject. We relate to each other and have a bigger connection because we've all experienced it. I'm doing everything I can to minimize the number of assaults and I'm hoping to use my education to help.

Dabney: Domestic violence against women of color and Native women especially in Alaska has crazy high statistics. I think there can be so many reasons why it's so prevalent in village life—they don't have jobs, they are fisherman and stuff like that. The lack of things to do and alcohol is a bad combination. They're not living 100 percent in a Native way anymore, and their priorities have been altered. They maybe have peace officers but not police. A lot of people will call for help, but when it gets down to prosecution, if they don't want to deal with it anymore, they just move on. If they don't want to charge their partner, nothing happens so it just repeats. They say "I still love this person even though he tried to hurt me."

Maria: Poverty is something that needs change. People are just stuck in the cycle of addiction and staying on the reservation where it's already poor. Your parents were in poverty so it's like you're stuck, you can't go to college or get out of it. And there are other things, like you'll have babies and then that costs a lot of money so you can't finish school. I think in order to get out of the cycle there needs to be more education! If you can't even finish high school, what kind of job are you going to get?

← **Emily:** It's bittersweet to talk about, because I fundamentally believe in the spirituality and traditional ways, respecting the environment and not wasting things—and I'm so proud of those core things—but then when I go back home to the reservation, what do I see? Everything's broken. It's heartbreaking. Now I see it in an even brighter light because I have my kids. I try and teach the kids to be proud of those ideas, but they see it too. When we go back to the reservation, they're like, how come there are those houses without front doors?

→ **Sharon:** How do we address the barriers of drugs and alcohol and the family? You can't just take a child out for a half-hour sit-down therapy session, because they still go back home and see those negative things and learn from them. We need to educate the family with coping skills instead of drugs and alcohol. I don't believe half-hour sessions will fix the kids. We've got to fix the family first.

Chelsey: In my culture, we tend to share and trade food. We hunt, and I like that because it's not processed by manufacturers that add GMO's to it! I just love Native food. We use it to help us do everything, and to stay warm. When I came to FLC from Alaska, there was a long period of time where my appetite was growing, I wasn't satisfied with the food that I bought. It bugged me. I talked with my parents, and they said "You need Native food! You need moose and fish!" The difference in purity helps out a lot.

Emily: People are so unhealthy back home, what they eat for everyday meals is heartbreaking to me. Coming here, everyone is really active and healthy. I think a lot of it is people see fast food as a cheap meal, and the resources for buying healthy food aren't there. In Alaska, produce and veggies are a lot more expensive. Fast food is a cheap way to feed your family. Education in schools about nutrition isn't there.

← **Trey:** We make our ancestors seem like saints, but they were human too. We're making our own propaganda about them and how amazing they were, but they weren't infallible because they stood up to Europeans. They were humans, with all of the faults that entails. I don't venerate them for their resistance. To a lot of people living today, that is all being Native means, to oppose or simply not associate with being white. It's a dichotomy that damages our ability to empathize and accept our fellow man.

→ **Brittany:** I'm passionate about lack of representation in mainstream media. That's my goal, it's what I live for! I want to be on CNN. When you think about current media, there aren't enough brown faces, so our Native children can't see a higher expectation for themselves, other than being a mom. If there was more of a representation of Natives that were proud and passionate on TV, it would have a bigger influence on the world. They'd see us in the higher ranks and they'd say "You're brown, it's possible!" When there's not, it just doesn't seem like it's within reach.

Joseph: I don't know how many times I've shaken my head this semester learning more about Native histories—the consistency of bad things in Native history is crazy. It leads up to now, things are still happening and some of them didn't happen that long ago! It blows me away. How can we claim to be such a great country that accepts everybody? The way that things were handled is just wrong. How were people that evil?

———————————————————————————————

Juliane: I initially felt both empowered and horrified after learning the histories of American Indian peoples. Learning these histories as an adult made me feel as if knowledge was purposefully hidden from me as a child in school.

Brandon: Culture should be important to students. Instead of talking about European cultures that changed the United States, talking about the people that were here first is really important. There was so much culture before Europeans came.

← **Nina:** I think all Native Americans should get free tuition no matter what school they go to! Wherever they're accepted to, they should be able to go there. I had to move away from my Native community to get my education here, and when I'm done I'm going back to my friends and family. How much good is it doing Native kids to have to leave solid supportive communities and come somewhere that they don't know? My community at home gets mad at me, like why are you leaving? They look at me kind of as a traitor! I'm slightly shunned because they're like "We'll be here, you'll just leave—fine." They were really disappointed.

→ **Christina:** In South Dakota, I went to a Lakota Catholic high school. It started more Catholic, but we said "That's not going to thrive here because they're going to kill our culture!" Now they added the Lakota part where they do morning prayer, so you take Lakota classes and then you take Jesus classes. You're required to do both. In the mass, there's a drum group in the opening, and then the priest comes in and he'll do his Catholic thing, and then parts are in Lakota. The Jesus classes are more like information and less telling us what to do.

Agatha: I'm surprised at how many Natives I see on campus. Where I'm from, they push college on you and everything but in the back of everybody's mind they're thinking "That person is going to fail. Natives are going to fail." I put off college a long time because I thought I would end up failing, so why even try? I just missed learning and challenging myself, and I ended up surprising myself when I came here because my first year I got all A's and B's.

Bree: In high school, I didn't do the best, so I had a lot of people telling me I couldn't do it, so I started to believe it. When I transferred to the school on the res I did a lot better and I had a lot of support. A lot of people are proud of me and they say "You're doing such a great thing!" I'm pretty proud of myself. I honestly didn't think I was smart enough and I didn't think I could afford to go to college until I heard about the waiver. There were seventeen kids in my graduating class and two of us went to college. I wasn't at the top of my class but here I am! When I get my degree, I'll go home and teach.

← **Daeja:** My family is so excited to hear about my experiences in college! They're always checking up and making sure that I'm fine and that I stay with it. My niece calls me, she's nine, and she says "Auntie, I want to be just like you—go to school, get a degree, and be a teacher!" It's nice to inspire and be the first one to do something no one else has done. But it's also scary, because everyone's watching you, so you have to be careful with everything you do!

→ **Michelle:** I was the oldest child so my mom expected me to go off to college. She was the first one in my family to go to college, so she was like "You're going to college, get your masters, get your PhD," all of that! I was the only one of my friends who actually did go to college. In high school, there were fifty of us incoming freshman in the Native All Nations program, and only about eight of us graduated. Everyone else would drop out or go to an alternative school.

Gabrielle: All of the cultural background that I have, I learned at home. When I came to college, I felt immersed in the culture because there is a lot more Native things happenings here. It's the first time I've seen more than a few Native people in my life, but I'm not full blood and I didn't live on the res, so I feel like I can't go to the Native activities here because I don't look Native and I'd get looks.

← **Mitchell:** Last year I went to the national conference for AISES [American Indian Science and Engineering Society]. It's really cool and in different locations every year. Natives from all over the country come and you meet a lot of Natives you'd never ever get a chance talk to otherwise. We're all STEM majors and you network a lot with big companies. There's a full-day career fair, you know, Boeing, Intel, NASA, and they bring the Natives that work there to talk to us. It's so cool having Natives at NASA trying to recruit you and tell you to apply for internships!

→ **Keyah:** I'm having to balance being Native with being a student, and it feels like two different things. There are bigger issues that I'm trying to focus on than trying to write a paper! I can either help my people or I can write this paper that's due tomorrow. So, it's a big trade-off in what I think is important. It's kind of like a divide I've always felt—I can be Native and have American Indian Studies as my major and work on the reservation, or I can just live in the white world and have a normal chemistry job. I feel like I have to pick my people, or a more "normal" job and future.

Thomas: I do a lot of work with MPIRG [Minnesota Public Interest Research Group] and often times what they'll do with racial justice issues is they'll separate people into groups based on whether you're a person of color or not. They do it so people can feel comfortable. Where to place myself in that matrix is very strange. For me to enter into a space for people of color when I don't look like at all like a person of color . . . even my appearance could be threatening to somebody, or would make somebody uncomfortable—it's an odd place to be. That terminology of the person of color is flawed and problematic! There's more to ethnicity than skin color. Though there are prejudices that you can face based on skin color certainly, that doesn't encompass everyone's experiences. One thing that I've been thinking about for MPIRG is a mixed race or passing area where people who don't necessarily feel 100 percent comfortable in either group could potentially move to. We've done it at times in the past, but even that is a strange thing to press on. What a bizarre world we've all created for ourselves! Maybe the problem is that we want so badly to put everything into boxes. We want so badly to simplify things and the fact of the matter is that everything is just really, really complicated. No matter how many labels you try to put on something it's never going to describe it just right. Nothing, ever.

Aspen: I don't know if I should call myself white or American Indian because I'm not totally either. I'm proud to be both and I don't want to just emphasize one. I love how rich our culture is and how peaceful. I see it as very beautiful.

← **Raine:** I love our culture and our language! Our feast is also really unique, no other tribe does that. But, I don't like the stereotypes about Natives and the fact that people think we're drunks or not educated.

→ **Arica:** The biggest thing for me is practicing art, I take it really seriously. Some people dance, some focus on language, but I don't think anyone worked on Native art like I did where I'm from. I argue with my teacher a lot about the rules of traditional art, though. I think once you're in art for a long time and understand the traditional ways, you can start bending the rules a little bit. So, I had to master traditional ways first, then I could start using other colors and other styles.

Mariah: Something that I'm really excited about with the overall indigenous community is indigenous feminism. A lot of women and men are trying to get back to that feminist train of thought. I know feminism is a Western term, but Native women were held in really high regards in their communities before colonization. Trying to reclaim that power is exciting.

Kai: I think one of my favorite parts about being Native is the ideology in my tribe. It's more run by women than men, so it was really accepting of breaking America's typical gender roles. Being a two-spirit or along those lines in my tribe was a really good thing, even though it's heavily looked down upon in American culture.

← **Terry:** I like the bear dance, that's my favorite thing. The story behind it and the purpose is awesome. I'm a firm believer in it. The story goes, this man has a vision while he's walking in the mountains, he hears this music and he walks over and there's a bear line dancing, essentially. The bear tells him everything the dance stands for and shows him the dance and the man takes it back to his tribe. It's a Ute tradition, and it's a celebration of Spring and the life that comes with it. You can't do it with anyone who you're dating or related to, so it's a good way to meet someone too!

→ **Terri:** I like to watch the dancing and the pageantry of powwows.

Dani: I love the culture, how Native Americans lived in the past and how they've been able to uphold a lot of their traditions in modern times. I wish I knew more specifics about my own tribe, though. My dad, who is Native, never told us much about it. I would probably go more the book route to learn.

Taylor: I don't even know my whole background. My parents just pretty much told me I'm Navajo. I've never traced anything back for myself because until recently I've never been asked to explain that before. My grandpa is a medicine man so he's like "Well, we did this. We went up and we came back down, we settled here." And I'm like, okay, where did you get that answer from? I question him and I'm like, I probably shouldn't be doing this, but I want to know.

_____

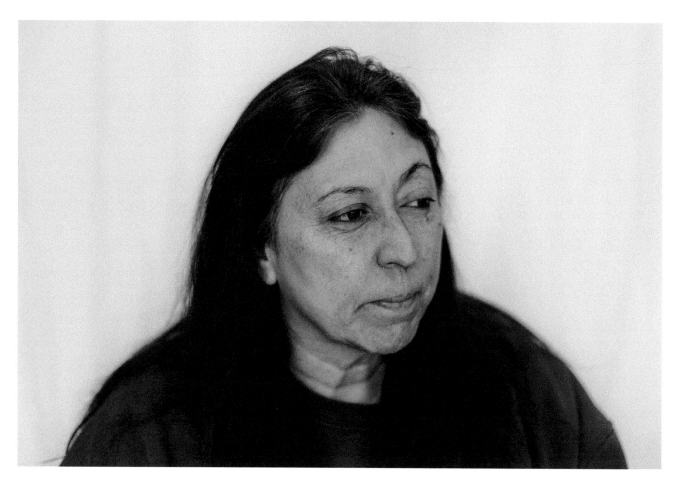

Mary Kay: My dad was in a boarding school and he didn't share a lot of experiences with us. I think he sheltered us because of what he went through as a child, so now my big interest is to find out as much as I can about it. He didn't share, but I want to know! I often wonder why my dad did the things he did . . . we could never spend a night away from home and we always needed to be in his sight. I thought that was so wrong because my friends got to do different things . . . but now I know he was protecting us. He'd always tell us, "My kids are never going to have to go through what I went through as a child."

Courtney: I'm trying to become more traditional. My grandparents were both in boarding schools and they don't want anything to do with it, so I'm trying to piece it together myself, and learn from others. My grandma refuses to talk about her time in the boarding school except to say she was there. My grandpa doesn't say anything. I didn't even know he was in a boarding school until my mom told me a few years ago. As time has progressed and being Native has become more popular, my grandma decided it's okay to be Native. She's like following the crowd, my mom actually at one point asked my grandma what my band was and my grandma said Oglala, but she lied. I'm actually another band, but she picked Oglala because it's the most popular of the bands.

Sara: I like being Native but I wish I knew more about the culture and history. My grandpa lives on the White Earth reservation but he doesn't practice any lifeways so we don't have much of that perspective.

_____

Natasha: They're sticking us in the past and we're still here, we've always been here and we'll always be here. I am proud of my culture, it's who I am. I am learning more and more about my Native heritage every day and it's an awesome feeling.

Monica: Now that I'm learning more about the social issues going on in Indian country, I understand the context but I know I have limited power where I am right now. But it's also motivating because I'm getting an education and I'll be armed with the tools to make change happen. It's like we are challenging the system being here!

Jonathan: When I was nineteen, a natural phenomenon happened that made me get appointed to being a tribal elder. Kind of like how it's so rare to get struck by lightning, it was that kind of thing. I uphold that position now, which was not what I asked for, but I was chosen. Since then I've been thinking, why? They said try to have a normal life, but what's a normal life? I feel upset about the fact that I can't go out and make mistakes and learn from it, I kind of have to watch what I do. Having to give up certain things, and having to balance the traditional and contemporary worlds is tough. From my standpoint as a tribal elder, I feel the whole world on my back knowing that I have to get a quality education to get a good future, and also having to get educated in my culture, my language, these practices in order to keep the culture alive. It gets overwhelming at times. But it's not about switching, it's about balancing.

Michael: I don't drink, I don't smoke. It helps me identify better as a strong Native male. How can we be taken seriously, as Native American scholars especially, if we are doing that stuff? Some Natives are so smart and can talk your ear off about federal Indian policy and can jam out a ten-page paper in ten minutes that's so articulate and well written, but yet, behind closed doors they're drinking a lot, or smoking a lot, and filling that void with whatever they need to. We need to get back to our ancestors' way of living, to have a clear mind and to walk in beauty as we call it.

Stephanie: My pursuit of being a Native scholar is to encourage and remind my fellow Native youth that we're the proof of resilience and that we have the opportunity now that our generations before us didn't. We really need to take it by the horns and just move! I almost feel like we're getting ready for a huge movement. We're preparing ourselves and our children to be great. There is no time to look at one another and put each other down because of the way we grew up or the opportunities we did or didn't have. At this point in my life, as I move forward, I'm grabbing hands with me and making sure that we're all moving together.

Answer Key

pages 30–31

Jessie: I feel kind of like a traitor when I go to powwows, because I'm Native but I'm also white. I don't "look" Native.

Carolyn: I feel like if I do tell people I'm Native, they're going to ask me about my culture, and I have no idea. I feel like I should find out more and get involved with Native life on campus, but I'd be worried about reactions to my fair skin in those circles.

Zachary: I feel proud to be Native, but I do not feel like I look it. I feel a little guilty when talking to "more pure" Native Americans regarding my relationship to being Native. I just enjoy my Native side, even looking dominantly white.

Devon: I'm quick to tell others about my Native identity, because it's who I am.

pages 56–57

Kellie: The questions aren't "Tell us about your culture," they're "Tell us what you gain monetarily from it?"

Jenny: I have to specify what kind of Indian I am. They assume "red dot." One of my friends thought that I was from India for a really long time.

Ashleigh: I've heard that because I'm a Native woman I couldn't be trusted. People have made alcoholism jokes, tuition waiver jokes, free money jokes. I wish I could educate the public better and fight racism and stereotypes.

Rachel: I'm from a tribe in the Vermont area. All of my best girl friends were Menomonie, but they just saw me as a white friend.